The Halloween Book

by Sharon & David

illustrated by Marilyn Mets

SOMERVILLE HOUSE PUBLISHING
Toronto

Canadian Cataloguing in Publication Data

McKay, Sharon, E.
        The Halloween book and pumpkin carving kit

ISBN 1-895897-05-X

1. Halloween decorations - Juvenile literature.
2. Jack-o-lanterns - Juvenile literature.
3. Halloween - Juvenile literature. I. MacLeod,David, 1953-.
II. Mets, Marilyn. III. Title.
TT900.H32M35 1994   j745.594'1   C94-930180-9

Printed in China.

Book Design by Marilyn Mets
Package Design by M and Y, Inc.
Industrial Design by Up Workshop
Edited by Jennifer Glossop

Published in the United States by Andrews and McMeel.

Published by Somerville House Publishing,
a division of Somerville House Books Limited
3080 Yonge Street, Suite 5000
Toronto, Ontario
M4N 3N1

Somerville House Publishing gratefully acknowledges the continued support of the Ontario Publishing Centre,
the Ontario Arts Council, the Ontario Development Corporation and the Department of Communications.

Dedication: To Stirling and Tory – S. & D.
        To the only pumpkin head I know... Tom – M.M.

Answers to Play it Safe, page 41

1. Adults should ask other adults – not children – for help. Walk away.

*2. Do not go into anyone's home for any reason. If you must go to the bathroom, it's
time to return home.*

3. Politely say no and leave.

*4. Walk up to the nearest lit house and ask the person in the house to call your
parents. Do not enter the house.*

5. Take your friend straight home.

*Remember, it's important to trick-or-treat in your own neighborhood. Stay close to
home.*

Contents

How Did Halloween Get Started?

About two thousand years ago, the Celts – people who lived in Great Britain and Ireland – celebrated a holiday they called Samhain (pronounced "Sa-wan"), named after the god of death. They believed that every year on the last day of October – when the harvest season had ended and the days were getting shorter and colder – the god Samhain allowed the souls of the dead to visit the homes they once lived in.

It was a scary time for the Celts. On that one night they left their homes and gathered in a field. There they built a huge bonfire to scare away all the evil spirits and any ghosts, goblins, or other demons that might be roaming about.

This holiday was the ancestor of our Halloween. But it wasn't called Halloween at first. When the Romans conquered the Celts in the first century A.D., they added parts of two of their festivals: Feralia, which was held to honor the dead, and Poloma, named after the Roman goddess of fruit and trees.

Time marched on. The Celt religion was replaced by Christianity. Sometime around A.D. 800, the Christian church declared November 1 as All Saints' Day to honor all the saints who did not have a special day of their own. People made their old customs from Samhain and the Roman festivals part of the new All Saints' Day rituals. The church also made November 2 All Souls' Day to honor the dead.

The mass said on All Saints' Day was known as Allhallowmas. The evening before, October 31, became known as All Hallow Even. Over time this name was shortened to Halloween.

The Bat Utensils

The Bat Utensils that came with your Halloween Book will help you carve your pumpkin. The Big Bat is the carver. It cuts lines. The two Baby Bats are punches. They make holes.

To make a face, pick one of the stencil shapes from the back of the book. Cut it out and place it on your pumpkin. Then punch holes along the stencil line. Remove the stencil. Use the Big Bat to cut a line that connects the holes.

Or you can you can draw shapes on your pumpkin with a marker. Use the Baby Bats to punch a hole in the pumpkin. Then use the Big Bat to cut out the shapes.

Remember to use your Bat Utensils only when an adult is with you and to make holes and cuts carefully. When you are finished, wash the utensils and put them away for the next year.

This is the adult's help needed symbol. If it appears beside an activity you choose to do, find an adult to do the activity with you.

Jack-o'-Lanterns

Meet Jack.

According to Irish legend, there once was a fellow named Jack who had a bad habit of playing nasty tricks on the devil. When Jack grew old and died, heaven would not let him in because he had not been a very good person. Besides, he had hung out with a bad crowd – the devil and pals. The devil did not want Jack either because Jack had played too many tricks on him. Jack had nowhere to go. He was forced to wander the earth forever. To light his way, Jack carved a lantern from a turnip. Inside the turnip, he placed a burning lump of coal he had stolen from the devil.

Our jack-o'-lanterns are descended from Jack's turnip!

Say Hello to Your Pumpkin

Get to know your pumpkin before you carve it up. Look at it. Is it lean and mean? Fat and jolly? Squat and pudgy, or short and puny?

Listen. Is your pumpkin crying out "I'm sad"? Is it yelling "Give me a scaaary face"? Does it positively scream "Make me too silly for words"? Didn't you know pumpkins can talk? This is Halloween, after all. Anything can happen.

★ Give your pumpkin a quick cleanup by wiping it with a damp cloth. Pat it dry. Place it on several sheets of newspaper.

★ Draw a circle around the stem with a marker. Holding the large Bat Carver so it points to the center of the pumpkin (otherwise the top might fall into the pumpkin), cut along the line. Lift off the top.

8

★ Reach inside the pumpkin and pull out the slippery gunk with your bare hands. Separate the seeds and save them for snacks (see page 30). Scrape out all the hanging bits with the spoon until the inside is smooth.

★ Now – create a masterpiece. Remove the stencils from the back of the book. Look at the faces in the Pumpkin Gallery on pages 10 to 13. Pick one of those for your pumpkin, or mix and match eyes, a nose, and a mouth.

★ Once you have decided which features to use, hold the stencil on the pumpkin and punch a dot-to-dot pattern with the Baby Bat. Remove the stencil. Then cut out the feature with the Big Bat carver. (Make sure they are not too close together, otherwise the face might collapse.)

(see page 30)

A Refreshing Dip

Is your pumpkin looking a tad tired and shriveled? Plunge it into cool water for a few minutes – not much longer or your pumpkin will get mushy.

To make your pumpkin last a little longer, mist it with lemon juice.

The Pumpkin Gallery

Light Your Pumpkin

You can choose spotlights, flashlights, or candles to light your pumpkin and bring a glow to its face.

FLASHLIGHTS

Flashlights are the safest way to light a pumpkin.

★ In the back of the pumpkin, carve a hole the same size around as the end of your flashlight. Put the flashlight through and turn it on. To get different colors from a flashlight, first cover the lens with colored cellophane.

SPOTLIGHTS

Spotlights come in different colors and will dazzle trick-or-treaters.

★ In the bottom of the pumpkin, carve a hole that is slightly larger around than the spotlight. Put the spotlight on the ground where no one can trip or stumble over the electrical cord. Lower the pumpkin so that the spotlight fits inside the hole.

Spotlights can get hot, so be careful when you're touching them.

CANDLES

★ Keep the candle upright by placing it in a candle holder small enough to fit in the pumpkin. Or, with an adult's help, drip a little candle wax on a plate small enough to fit through the hole in the pumpkin. Stick the bottom of the candle into the hot wax. Wait until the wax on the plate hardens. Then lower the candle holder or plate into the pumpkin.

★ Place the pumpkin away from curtains, decorations, or anything else that could catch on fire. If the pumpkin is outdoors, it should be kept well away from trick-or-treaters who may have costumes that could burn. And keep it well off the path and away from the door.

★ Once your pumpkin is in place, ask an adult to light the candle for you.

PAINTING PUMPKINS

If you would rather not carve and light your pumpkin, paint it instead.

You will need:
• Pumpkin
• Newspaper
• Marker or pen
• Paints (tempera or acrylic)
• Paintbrushes

★ Wash your pumpkin and dry it well. Place it on the newspaper. Turn your pumpkin around and look at it from all sides. Is there a design that springs to mind?

★ With a marker or pen, sketch your design directly on the pumpkin. Begin painting with the darkest color first. Since you may have to let one color dry before using a second or third, keep your project in a place where it can remain untouched for a few days.

All Dressed Up

What to wear? Costumes are as much a part of Halloween as pumpkins.

Are you heading out for an evening's trick-or-treating? If you live in a cold climate, you need an oversized costume that covers a jacket or warm sweater.

Perhaps you're off to a party? Then you'll want a costume that won't fall apart.

Maybe you'll be wearing the costume at school first, then to trick-or-treat? You'll want a really sturdy costume.

Where can you find your costume? Do you have a costume box? Rummage away. Check out your local second-hand clothing store. Think about your own clothes. Do you have a black-and-white striped shirt and black pants? Great, you have the makings of a zebra. Add a tail and ears, and paint black-and-white stripes on your face–and you're ready! Do you have an extra-large man's shirt? You have the beginnings of a hobo, or a clown, or a headless man. Your imagination is the only limit.

Why not wake up a sleeper? Pajama sleepers not only make the base of great costumes, they also are fire-retardant. With your parents' permission, you may want to cut off the feet or use a footless sleeper.

As for your feet, running shoes are best.

A word of warning: Do not pillage your parents' closets without their permission. Some parents have been known to get a bit grumpy when they discover that their clothes are about to take a walk around the neighborhood without them.

Whose Face Is That?

Makeup is better than a mask for disguising yourself. You can't lose it, and it's safer, since it doesn't block your vision. You can buy face paints at the store.

ABOUT FACE PAINTS

Choose water-based face paints. Avoid the grease sticks actors use. (They are oil-based and hard to remove.)

Before you use any makeup, test it on a small patch of skin, perhaps on the inside of your arm or wrist. Leave it for a few hours to see if a rash appears. If it does, or your skin gets itchy, don't use the makeup.

PERFECT MAKEUP

★ Clean your face and hands. Apply a thin layer of face cream. This will make it easier to take the makeup off later.

★ Apply a base coat of makeup using your fingers or a small sponge. Let the first coat dry before you add different colors of paint. Avoid putting makeup near your eyes.

★ To make lines, use a small brush or a Q-Tip.

★ To remove makeup, wash your face with soap and water.

★ One last thing: Clean up afterward.

ACCESSORIES

Old coffee grounds stuck to the chin make great beard stubble. Press the coffee grounds into the face paint while it is still moist.

You can also "glue" bits of paper to your face. Simply cut a raw potato in half. Rub the cut surface on a small decal such as a paper heart or star. Stick the decal on your face. This natural glue lasts an hour or so.

*Six Simply Smashing Costumes

Want to make your own costume? Here are six you can make with a minimum of fuss and bother. Ask a grown-up to help you, however.

*Note to Parents:
All the costumes in this book are suitable for boys and girls and take safety into account. They all use materials found around the home or in any small department store. Sleepers, jogging suits, or pajamas are suggested as a base in many of the costumes but are not necessary.

LITTLE DEVIL

You will need:
- Red jogging pants and red turtleneck (or a red sleeper)
- Plastic headband
- 1 yard (1 m) red felt
- Fabric glue or needle and thread
- Cotton stuffing
- Red or black hat
- Safety pins
- Reflective tape

★ Put on the pants and turtleneck (or the sleeper).

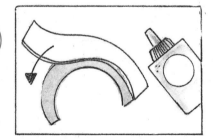

★ Cut a strip of red felt the same size as the headband. Glue it on top of the headband.

★ For the devil's horns, cut two 3-inch (8 cm) diamond shapes out of the felt. Fold each diamond into a triangle. Put some cotton stuffing inside. Sew or glue the edges together. Glue the folded end of each horn to the headband.

★ Put on the hat. Slide headband on top.

★ For the devil's tail, cut a strip of red felt about 1 foot (30 cm) long and 5 inches (13 cm) wide. Fold in half lengthwise. Sew down the length of the felt. Stuff with cotton stuffing.

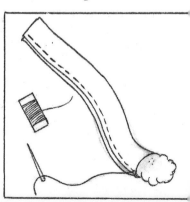

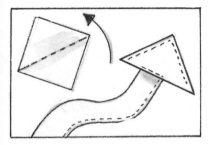

★ Cut a square 4 inches (10 cm) wide out of the felt. Fold tip to tip to form a triangle. Sew, leaving a small opening to stuff. Stuff. Sew up the opening. Stitch the triangle to the end of your tail. Pin tail to back of pants.

★ Stick reflective tape on your costume.

Makeup
You will need:
• Red, black, and gold face paint; a small paintbrush.

★ Cover your face with a base coat of red. (Be careful around your eyes.)

★ Outline your eyes and eyebrows with black.

★ Paint a black goatee on your chin.

★ Paint your lips black.

★ Use the paintbrush to paint gold flames up the sides of your face.

★ Paint your eyelids gold.

LADYBUG

You will need:
- Red pants and top (or a red sleeper)
- 6 squares 4-inch x 4-inch (10 cm x 10 cm) black felt
- Safety pins or needle and thread
- Red hat
- Black earmuffs
- Reflective tape

★ Put on the pants and top (or the sleeper).

★ Cut the black felt squares into circles. Pin or loosely stitch five circles to the back of your top or sleeper. Pin one to the front to cover your tummy.

★ Put on the red hat. Slide on earmuffs from the back of your head pointing upwards. (These are the ladybug's antennae.)

★ Stick reflective tape on your costume.

Makeup

You will need:
- Red and black face paint

★ Cover your face with a base coat of red. (Be careful around your eyes.) Paint your neck and chin black.

★ Paint a thick black line down the middle of your face. Mark three black dots on each side of your face.

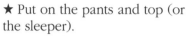

CUDDLY RABBIT

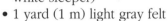

You will need:

- White or gray jogging suit (or a white sleeper)
- 1 yard (1 m) light gray felt
- Safety pins, fabric glue, or needle and thread
- 1 foot (30 cm) white fake fur or 1 bag cotton balls
- Headband
- Tape or stapler
- 1 sheet white or pink poster or bristol board
- 1 ball pink or white wool
- Reflective tape

★ Put on jogging suit or sleeper.

★ Cut a piece of felt the size of your tummy. Pin, glue, or stitch it on the front of your clothes.

★ Cut two bunny ear shapes out of the bristol board. Cut two pieces of fake fur slightly smaller than the ears. Glue fake fur or cotton balls to the "insides" of the ears.

★ Tape or staple the ears to the headband.

★ For the tail, stitch on a small ball of loosely wound white wool onto your behind.

★ Stick reflective tape on your costume.

Makeup
You will need:

- White, black, red, and pink (mix red and white) face paint

★ Paint large white circles around your eyes. Outline the circles in black.

★ Cover the rest of your face with pink makeup.

★ Draw red hearts on both cheeks.

★ Paint the space between your mouth and nose white and draw on some black whiskers and black freckles.

★ Paint the tip of your nose black.

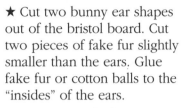

BUMBLEBEE

You will need:

- Yellow top and pants (or a yellow sleeper)
- Black electrical tape
- 1 sheet black poster or bristol board
- Fabric glue or large safety pins
- Yellow hat
- Black headband
- Reflective tape

★ Put on the top and pants (or the sleeper).

★ Cut black electrical tape into strips, and wrap them around your body.

★ Fold bristol board in half. Cut wings as shown. Pin or glue the wings on your back.

★ Put on the hat and put headband over it. Presto – a yellow head with a big black stripe.

★ Stick reflective tape on your costume.

Makeup

You will need:

- Yellow and black face paint

★ Cover your face with a base coat of bright yellow.

★ Paint black circles around your eyes.

★ Paint your lips black.

★ Draw black antennae above each eye.

SKELETON

You will need:

- Black turtleneck and tights
- Boy's white bathing suit (or similar garment)
- White adhesive tape
- White bathing cap
- Reflective tape

★ Dress in black from head to toe. Pull on the boy's white bathing suit over the black tights. This is for the big white hip bones of the skeleton.

★ Cut 12-inch (30 cm) lengths of adhesive tape. (Keep your scissors handy to trim the tape as you go.) Stick tape to body to make a skeleton. The diagram will guide you.

★ Put on the bathing cap.

★ Stick reflective tape on your costume.

Makeup

You will need:

- White and black face paint

★ Cover your face with a base coat of white.

★ Draw large black circles around your eyes. Outline your nose and lips with black.

★ Fill in the eye, lip, and nose area with black.

You will need:

- Extra-large black sweatshirt or turtleneck
- Black tights or pants
- Black bathing cap or hat
- 6 long cardboard tubes (from rolls of wrapping paper)
- 1 yard (1 m) black felt
- Fabric glue
- Stuffing (optional)
- Black elastic
- Needle and thread
- 3 small pillows
- Black belt
- Reflective tape

★ Dress in black from head to foot.

★ Cut the cardboard tubes the same length as your arm. Cut felt wide enough to go around the tubes and the same length as the tubes.

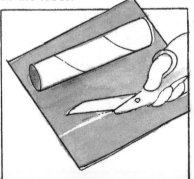

★ Wrap felt around the tubes and glue it in place. (To make the arms softer, forget about the cardboard tubes. Instead, sew the felt and stuff the "arms.")

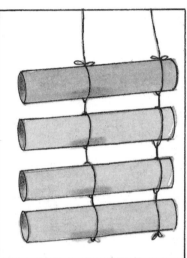

★ Lay three arms side by side about four inches (10 cm) apart. Tie black elastic around each arm at one end and again in the middle – see the diagram for help. Leave a 1-foot (30 cm) length at the end. Repeat with the other three arms.

★ Sew the end of each arm to the side of your top. Tie the loose ends of the elastic to your elbows and wrists.

★ If you want to be a fat spider, put a small pillow under your top. Hold it in place with a belt. Stuff the other two small pillows down your pants, one in front and one in back.

★ Stick lots of reflective tape on your costume.

Makeup

You will need:

- Light blue (mix dark blue and white) and black face paint; bright red lipstick

★ Paint your face light blue.

★ Draw large black ovals around each eye.

★ Color your lips with bright red lipstick.

Have a Wicked Party

Here are some ideas for planning a great Halloween party of your own.

PARTY THEMES

Give your party a theme.

Samhain: Dress up like Celts and Druids. Wear lots of fake furs and long dark robes. Make your home look like a forest.

Witches' Convention: Dress up like witches and warlocks. Decorate your home with broomsticks and cardboard black cats.

Pirate Ship: Dress up like pirates. Fly a flag with a skull and crossbones.

Ghost Get-together: Dress up like ghosts and zombies.

Zoo Bash: Dress up like animals. Put black strips of paper on the windows to look like bars.

Space Station Celebration: Dress up like weird space people.

Monster Meeting: Dress up like Frankenstein's monsters, mummies, and werewolves.

Costume-making Party: Ask your guests to come without disguises. Everyone makes his or her own costume and paints each other's faces. (Ask your guests' parents to send along old clothes for costume-making.)

AIRY INVITES

Blow up orange balloons but don't tie the end. Hold the end and write the invitation with black felt pen. Tell your guests what to bring and what to wear. Then let the air out and deliver.

BEWITCHING SOUNDS

Make a tape of scary sounds to play when your guests arrive. Here are some sounds you might include on your tape:
- high-pitched screams
- low-pitched moans
- rattling chains
- fingernails on a chalkboard
- a rainstorm (crinkle cellophane)
- wind (blow softly over the microphone)
- other spooky sounds like thumps, squeals, dragging feet and creaking doors.

IN THE DARK

Here are some ways to make your party room spooky.

Replace some or all of the bulbs in your light fixtures and lamps with colored lights. Blue and green give off eerie glows. Ultraviolet or "black" lights work well because the light they give off is faint and purplish. Keep the room dim, and provide just enough light to get around safely. Tip the pictures on the wall to give the room that off-balance feeling.

Things to Startle Your Friends

Fill the room with as many scary things as possible. Here are a few ideas.

COBWEBS

★ Hang damp black yarn or threads from the ceiling and doorway so that they brush against your friends as they walk into and around the room. (Keep safety in mind. Threads and yarn should just touch the tops of heads and not be long enough to go around people's necks.) Don't forget to mention that your pet tarantula got loose a few months back and you still haven't found it.

Fake Blood
Combine red food coloring with some clear corn syrup. Mix until you get the color and consistency you want. Be careful! Fake Blood will stain.

BODILESS ARM

★ Cut the sleeve off an old shirt and stuff it with rolled newspaper. Stick a stuffed glove in the cuff of the shirt. Cut a knife or hatchet out of cardboard and paint it. Make the glove grip it. For a ghoulish effect, cover the knife or hatchet and the shoulder end of the arm with fake blood (see box).

HEADLESS MAN

★ Find a box big enough for you to get inside and cut a head-sized hole in the top.

Use makeup to give yourself a really ghoulish face. Pull on the box and pop your head through the hole. Ask a friend to escort other pals into the room. When an unsuspecting person gets close, or shines a flashlight on your scary head, wait a second, then say, "BOOOOOOOOO!"

POLTERGEISTS

★ A poltergeist is a ghost who scares people by moving around furniture and objects. You can be a poltergeist. Tie some clear fishing line or thread to a few objects in the room. Maybe a chair leg. Or the door handle. Or a stick holding a briefcase open. Hide in the corner of the room holding the other end of the lines. (Make sure that nobody can trip over the lines.) When a guest gets near the object, pull the line and…WHOOSH-SLAM-BANG!…a poltergeist is playing a mischievous game again.

Haunted houses are lots of fun. Just remember: Play safe but think like a ghoul.

Fun and Games

Apples and fortune-telling have been the basis of Halloween since it began.

APPLE GAMES

Bobbing

★ Fill a big tub or sink with water and dump in lots of apples. With your hands behind your back, try to remove an apple with your teeth. If you want to make this game a little more spooky, add some yellow food coloring to the water and toss in a plastic frog and some plastic insects. Tell your guests that they are bobbing in bog water.

★ Or toss gummy worms into the bottom of the tub. Armed with a pair of tongs, go fishing for worms. Everyone gets to eat the worms they catch. Wet gummy worms are the slipperiest, slimiest things around. Yum, yum.

Snap Apple

★ Hang an apple from the ceiling on a long string. Set it swinging. Keeping your hands behind your back, try taking a bite from the apple.

FORTUNE TELLING

Apple Fortunes

★ Each guest chooses an apple. Cut it in half from top to bottom. Choose one half of the apple to tell the "real fortune" and the other to tell the "goofy fortune."

★ Count how many seeds you can see in the apple and tell the guest's fortune as follows. (When you're finished, eat the apples!)

REAL FORTUNE

1 seed	you will have same luck as last year
2 seeds	you will be lucky in love
3 seeds	you will receive lots of money
4 seeds	you will take a long trip
5 seeds	you will be happy in work
6 seeds	you will have good health
7 seeds or more	you will receive many blessings in life

GOOFY FORTUNE

1 seed	you will stub your toe
2 seeds	you will be kissed by a dog
3 seeds	you will find a nickel
4 seeds	you will walk to the store backward
5 seeds	you will do lots of chores
6 seeds	you will sneeze within two days
7 seeds or more	you will have luck every Tuesday

Marry Game

★ Peel an apple into one long peel. Spin the peel over your head until a piece breaks off. Look at the broken piece and decide which letter of the alphabet it looks like. The letter is the first initial of the person you will marry.

Marbles and Eyeballs

★ Fill a plastic bag with cold cooked spaghetti noodles. Add a handful of grapes. Presto – a bag of brains and eyeballs. Add four different-colored marbles to the bag. Mix well. Reach into the bag and feel around until you find a marble.

★ Your fortune depends on the color of the marble you pull out. Make up your own fortune for each color. If you pull out an eyeball (grape) by mistake…you have to eat it.

Red marble	fame and fortune await
Black marble	your brains are your fortune
Yellow marble	good times are coming
Green marble	your good heart will save the day

Goodies to Eat

Combine a willing parent or other big person with a fool-proof recipe and presto – a delicious dish.

ROASTED PUMPKIN SEEDS

- 2 cups (500 mL) pumpkin seeds
- 2 teaspoons (10 mL) salt

★ Mix seeds and salt. Spread on cookie sheet. Bake at 350°F (180°C) for 20 minutes. Cool and store.

★ To add zing, sprinkle seeds with a little chili powder or cajun pepper before baking.

★ To turn the pumpkin seeds bloody red or ghoulish green (this is Halloween, right?), sprinkle the seeds with 1 tablespoon (15 mL) strawberry or lime gelatin powder before baking.

PUMPKIN PARTY MIX

- 2 cups (500 mL) cereal (Chex, Shreddies, etc.)
- 1 tablespoon (15 mL) allspice
- 2 cups (500 mL) roasted pumpkin seeds

★ Mix cereal and allspice. Spread on cookie sheet. Bake at 200°F (100°C) for 10 minutes. Cool. Stir in roasted pumpkin seeds.

YEAH!!

CANDY APPLES

- 3/4 cup (175 mL) sugar
- 1/2 cup (125 mL) corn syrup
- 1/4 cup (50 mL) warm water
- Red food coloring
- 10 apples
- 10 Popsicle sticks

★ Combine sugar, corn syrup, and water in a heavy saucepan.

★ Cook over medium-low heat until sugar is dissolved. Raise heat to medium-high. Cook until heat registers 300°F (150°C) on a candy thermometer. (If you don't have a candy thermometer, drop a small amount of syrup into ice water. If it's hot enough, it will separate into hard brittle threads.)

★ Stir in red food coloring.

★ Poke a Popsicle stick into each apple. Carefully dip apples in the syrup. Stand the apples on wax paper to harden.

EYEBALL JELLY

Jelly that stares back at you. Dee-licious.

- Lemon gelatin
- 12 green grapes
- 12 raisins

★ Make lemon gelatin according to package instructions. Chill in the refrigerator for half an hour.

★ Peel grapes. Poke raisins into the grapes and press into the not-quite-set gelatin. Put the gelatin back in the fridge to finish setting.

PURPLE PUNCH

- 1/4 cup (50 mL) grape juice concentrate
- 1 26-ounce (750 mL) bottle club soda

★ Mix concentrate and soda in a punch bowl.

SPOOKY ICE CUBES

★ Put peeled green grapes in ice cube trays. Fill with water and freeze.

★ Add ice cubes to punch.

★ Serve in individual glasses with thick black licorice sticks.

Not Just an Ordinary Pumpkin

Here are some fancy ways to display your pumpkin.

You will need:
- Pumpkin
- Bat Utensils
- Old shoes, the bigger the better
- 2 Popsicle sticks or skewers
- Old gloves
- Hat

★ Carve a goofy pumpkin face. Rest the pumpkin on the shoes. Poke a stick in each side of the pumpkin. Hang gloves on the sticks. Top off with a silly hat.

PUMPKIN SPIDER

You will need:

- Small pumpkin
- Bat Utensils
- 4 wire coat hangers
- Black electrical tape or black ribbon
- Plastic bugs

★ Carve a spidery face in your pumpkin.

★ With an adult's help, cut the hangers at the "elbow" (see illustration) to make eight spider legs. Wrap each leg in electrical tape, sticky side up, or in ribbon. Poke each leg into the pumpkin. If you used electrical tape, the plastic bugs will stick to your pumpkin spider's legs.

VEGETABLE HEAD

You will need:

- Pumpkin
- Bat Utensils
- Vegetables
- Toothpicks

★ Carve a silly face on your pumpkin. Now add the vegetables, holding them in place with toothpicks. A carrot can be a nose. Radishes may be eyeballs. Grapes can be hair. Parsley might be a mustache. Use toothpicks to form eyebrows. Dill pickles turned up are smiling, turned down they are frowning. A large lettuce leaf may be hair, but placed under a pumpkin it may serve as a collar.

★ Put two cauliflower stalks touching end-to-end and – presto – a white bow tie. Small paper plates jammed into two slits on each side of the head are your pumpkin's ears. Go wild. Go wacky.

PUMPKIN DOLL

You will need:
- Lawn chair or sturdy wooden chair
- Old clothes: pants, shirt, hat, mittens, boots
- Newspaper

★ Choose the spot for the chair. It's hard to move a pumpkin doll.

★ Stuff old clothes with balled-up newspaper. Prop up the stuffed clothes in the chair to look like a person. If necessary, tie the clothes to the chair with cord. Position the boots under the chair.

★ Carve the pumpkin and prop it on top of the clothes. Will its head roll? We hope not. But if it does, run a broom handle down the shirt and into the ground. Now plop the pumpkin directly on the broom handle.

★ Use a flashlight – NOT candles – in this pumpkin.

SPIKY

This guy has a headache!

You will need:
- Pumpkin
- Bat Utensils
- "Spikes" – skewers or large nails or pipe cleaners

★ Carve a face in your pumpkin. Stick skewers, large nails, or pipe cleaners (or a combination) all around Spiky's head. You might need to make small holes for the pipe cleaners.

Want your pumpkin to smell? Sprinkle cinnamon or nutmeg on the underside of the lid. The candle or light will warm the spices and give off a delicious aroma.

35

SCARECROW PUMPKIN

Choose the spot for your pumpkin scarecrow. Will it stand in the middle of the lawn or sit in a chair by the door?

You will need:

- 2 pieces two-by-four, one about 6 feet (2 m) long, the other 4 feet (1.25 m)
- Hammer and nails
- Old pants
- 4 to 6 cornstalks or old rags for stuffing
- Old shirt
- Pumpkin

★ Put one piece of wood on top of the other as shown. Hammer the pieces together.

★ Put the long end into one leg of the pants.

★ Drive the long end into the ground. Let the pants fall to the ground.

★ Tie corn stalks to the wood. The stalks will fatten your scarecrow up a bit and peek through at the neck and wrists.

★ Pull the pants up over the corn stalks. Stuff the other leg with stalks. Pull the shirt sleeves over the shorter piece of wood and stuff with stalks or old rags.

★ Carve a face on your pumpkin. Cut a 2-inch x 4-inch (5 cm x 10 cm) hole in the bottom. Push the pumpkin head onto the top of the pole.

What a masterpiece!

Note: *It's safest to use flashlights – rather than candles – in pumpkins. With a pumpkin scarecrow, a flashlight is a must. NEVER use a candle.*

Show-offs

After all the effort that has gone into carving or painting your pumpkin, you want everyone to see it.

Maybe you have been very energetic and have carved lots of pumpkins. Or perhaps you have had a pumpkin-carving party and now have more pumpkins than you can shake a witch's broom at. Here are a couple of suggestions for what you might do with them all.

★ To make a pumpkin totem pole, you need something to hold three or more pumpkins on top of one another. Two ways to do this are with tomato cages and wooden stakes.

★ Tomato cages (which are sold in garden stores) are rings

of thin wire that help tomato plants stand up straight. The rings can also hold pumpkins in place. In the dark the wire is invisible and the totem appears to be standing on its own. Yikes!

★ Or take two wooden stakes and stick them into the ground. Plop the pumpkins on the stakes.

You will need:
• 3 or more carved pumpkins
• Spotlight
• Tomato cage or 2 wooden stakes

★ Cut holes in the tops and bottoms of all your pumpkins. The holes should be all the same size and at least as big as the spotlight.

★ Put the spotlight in place on the ground.

★ Place the tomato cage over the spotlight, pushing the wires deep into the ground. Or push the stakes into the ground on each side of the light.

★ Slide the pumpkins into the cage or lower them onto the stakes.

★ Turn on the light. It should shine upward and light all your pumpkins. Impressive!

PUMPKIN PARADE

You will need:

• String of outdoor Christmas tree lights
• 3 or more carved pumpkins

★ String the lights on the ground in a straight line near, but not too close to, a walkway or path.

★ Cut a hole in the bottom of each pumpkin. Plop each pumpkin on a different light on the string. Turn on the lights. You now have a pumpkin parade.

Halloween: The Big Day

Trick or treat,
Smell my feet,
Give me something
good to eat.

Halloween customs and rituals have developed slowly over time. The Scottish Celts used to parade with torches through their towns before lighting their bonfires. The Welsh used to make marks on stones before throwing them into the bonfire. (It was feared that anyone who could not find their stone the next morning would die within the year.)

The Irish would parade through the town asking for food in honor of one of their gods, Muck Olla.

Later, in England, Halloween was also known as Snap Apple Night. People would gather around a fire and tell tall tales while munching apples and nuts.

Halloween didn't really get started in North America until the 1800s, when a lot of immigrants arrived from Ireland, Scotland, and England and brought with them their Halloween customs.

Halloween, North American style, was not always a fun time. In the beginning of the twentieth century, Halloween was a time when people played pranks on one another.

When the pranks got out of hand, civic groups took Halloween out of the hands of the hooligans and gave it to the community. Soon, communities everywhere were celebrating with festivals, parties, and costume parades. Parks were decorated, contests arranged, and treats were provided for children.

Certain places revived the Celtic and English tradition of knocking on doors and asking for charity. This practice spread and developed into what we now know as trick-or-treating.

In the 1940s members of the Presbyterian church used trick-or-treating as an opportunity to collect money and clothing, which they sent to the United Nations for distribution to needy children. As a result, in 1946 the United Nations International Children's Emergency Fund (UNICEF) was founded. Children today are still using Halloween as a great opportunity to collect for UNICEF. (Check it out in your school.)

Halloween has taken a long time to evolve into what it is today, a time of magic, mystery, dress-up, and CANDY!

An Apple a Day

Have you ever received an apple in your loot bag? Did you get grumpy and think, "Hummm, I wish this was a candy"? Wish no more. The Celts believed that apples gave a person immortality. The next time you find an apple in your loot bag, you'll know that you've been given a good luck charm that brings with it a long and happy life.

WITCH

Witch, witch, where do you fly?
Over the moon, and under the sky.
Witch, witch, what do you eat?
Little black apples from Hurricane Street.
Witch, witch, what do you drink?
Vinegar, blacking,* and good red ink.
Witch, witch, where do you sleep?
Up in the clouds, where pillows are cheap.

* boot polish

40

Play It Safe

Maybe this is the year you and a buddy are planning to trick-or-treat. Here are some questions you may want to talk over with your parents. See if their answers match your own.

What would you do if:

1. A person stops his or her car and asks you for directions?

2. Whoops, you have to go to the bathroom while you're out trick-or-treating. What now?

3. A really nice person asks you to come into her or his house to show off your costume?

4. You get the streets mixed up and can't find your way home?

5. Your friend eats too much candy and gets sick?

These are tough questions. Turn to page 2 and check out the answers at the bottom .

Turn to page 2 and check out the answers at the bottom .

RULES OF THE ROAD

It's buddy-up time when you take to the streets,
But wait till you're home before tasting your treats.
Tell your folks of the route that you're planning to take,
Set a time to come home and be sure you're not late.
Don't enter a house – just politely say no.
And there's no need to talk to someone you don't know.
Avoid dogs and dark alleys and criss-crossing the street.
Stick to sidewalks or walk facing traffic you meet.
Carry flashlights or lamps to see where you are,
For a driver can't see a small ghost from her car.
So trick-or-treat safely and remember the rule:
Your very own instincts are your best safety tool.

We know that you know NOT to eat any candy from your loot bag before an adult has inspected it. To waylay a snack-attack, pack a treat from home and nibble as you go.

Loot

This year when you are shelling out goodies, think about things besides candy you can give out to trick-or-treaters:

* toothbrushes
* samples of toothpaste
* erasers
* 3 crayons tied together with ribbon
* pencils
* mini coloring books
* pads of paper

What if you can't eat candy? Set up a trading post with your friends the day after Halloween. Your friends can bring their comics or baseball cards to your house for a trading feast!

DID YOU KNOW?
In 1991, 6.4 million pounds (3 million kilograms) of candy was manufactured for Halloween. Yikes! Laid out in a straight line, the candy would make a ring around the world.
(National Confectioners Association)

Stencils

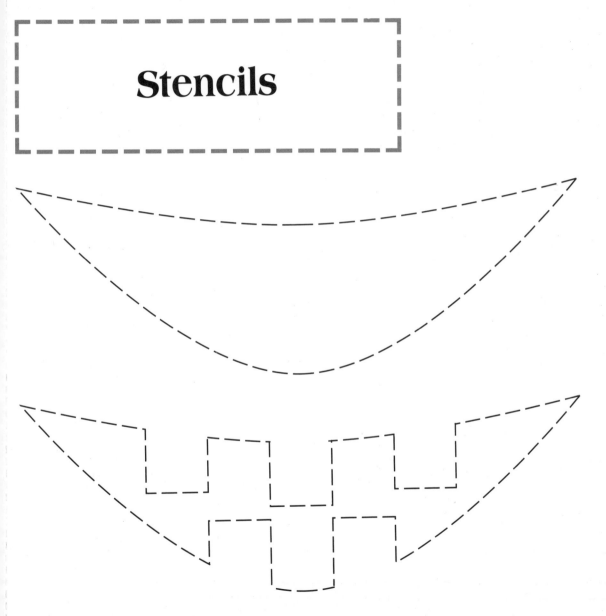

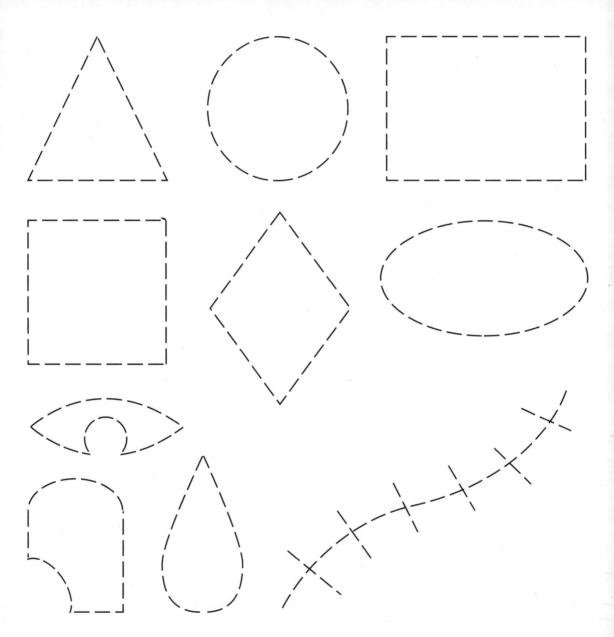

*T*he following books are available at good bookstores everywhere. If, however, they are not available at your local bookstore, you can order them directly from Somerville House Books Limited.

Quantity

The Bug Book and Bottle	$ 9.95	_____
The Bird Book and Bird Feeder	12.95	_____
The Beach Book and Beach Bucket	10.95	_____
The Garden Book and Greenhouse	12.95	_____
The Pond Book and Pail	12.95	_____
The Wildflower Field Guide and Press	13.95	_____
The Environmental Detective Kit	16.95	_____
The Pathfinder's Adventure Kit	15.95	_____
The Paper Book and Paper Maker	14.95	_____
The Make-Your Own Button Book	13.95	_____
Chalk Around the Block	9.95	_____
The Bones Book and Skeleton	17.95	_____
The Baseball Book and Trophy	13.95	_____
The Money Book and Bank	14.95	_____
The Lunch Book and Bag	12.95	_____
Brush Them Bright	10.95	_____
Lace Them Up	10.95	_____
The Tiny Perfect Dinosaur: Leptoceratops	14.95	_____
The Tiny Perfect Dinosaur: Tyrannosaurus Rex	14.95	_____
To The Limit	19.95	_____
Blue Planet	19.95	_____
The Dream is Alive	19.95	_____
The Kids' Soccer Book	11.95	_____
The Halloween Book and Pumpkin Carving Kit	11.95	_____
The Bones and Skeleton GameBook	9.95	_____
Henry's Moon	14.95	_____
Tyrannosaurus Rex Poster	14.95	_____
Changes in You and Me: A Book About Puberty – Mostly for Girls	14.95	_____
Changes in You and Me: A Book About Puberty – Mostly for Boys	14.95	_____

Order Total: _____
Plus 7% GST (Cdn. residents only): _____
Plus shipping and handling (in Canada add $4, in the U.S. add $5 per item ordered): _____

Total Enclosed: _____

Your Name: .... Address: ....

City: .... Province/State: .... Postal/Zip Code: ....Country: ....

Please send money order or certified cheque to: Order Department, Somerville House Books Limited, 3080 Yonge Street, Suite 5000, Toronto, Ontario, Canada M4N 3N1